PLAIN TO FANCY

THE STORY OF THE LAKE HOTEL

by Barbara Dittl and Joanne Mallmann

foreword by Horace Albright

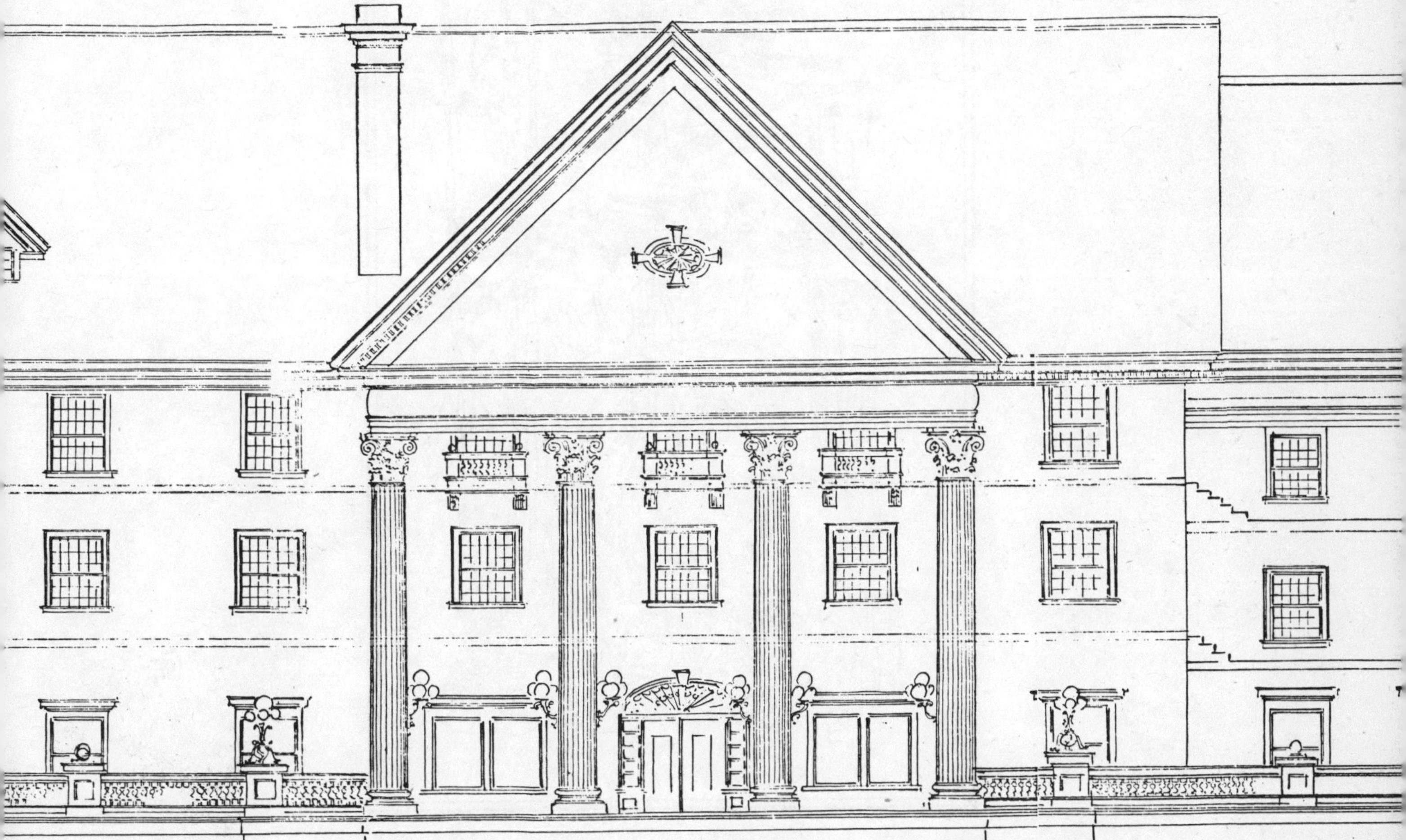

ROBERTS RINEHART, INC. PUBLISHERS

The pen and ink illustrations appearing in this book are an artist's interpretation of tile sections of the Robert Reamer designed fireplace and drinking fountain and Kersey carved glass panels installed at the Lake Hotel.

Published by Roberts Rinehart, Inc. Publishers
Post Office Box 3161 Boulder, Colorado 80303
International Standard Book Number 0-911797-31-9

Lake Hotel porte cochere, 1925. Courtesy of the Haynes Foundation Collection, Montana State Historical Society

Preface and Acknowledgments

TEN YEARS ago the history of the Lake Hotel was hand written on a 3 × 5 inch index card taped next to the cash register in the building's dining room. We read the words, "Built in 1889, major additions in 1923 and 1928; architect unknown." Our initial interest in who designed the structure and how much paint it took to cover it (500 gallons) developed into a project that traces the social and architectural history of Yellowstone's oldest hotel from 1889 to its centennial.

OUR THANKS to the following people who shared their time and memories of the Lake Hotel with us. Horace M. Albright, John Albright, Richard Bartlett, Jerry Bateson, Sr., Val Black, Glenda Bradshaw, John Burchill, Huntley Child, Jr., Berle Clemensen, Mary Shivers Culpin, Maryann Davis, John Delmar, Curt Edlund, Dick and Rosemary Engle, Jean Galusha, Newell Gough, Aubrey Haines, Tom Hallin, Mark Hargis, Julie Hauser, Julie Hayes, Isabel M. Haynes, Charlie Hudson, Steve Kersey, John King, Larry Kreisman, Bill Lang, David Leavengood, Tim

Manns, Verne Moss, Adeline Moulton, Tom Nelson, Tom Overturf, Minnie Paugh, Herbert Peck, Ellie and Trevor Povah, Harry Rhodda, Marion Child Sanger, Marian Albright Schenck and Ros Schenck, Laurence Schilla, Scotty, Ruby Shields, Dave Smith, George Swim, Steve Tedder, Dave Walter, Jean Ward, Mark Watson, Rodd Wheaton, Jane Reamer White, Bev Whitman, Lee Whittlesey. And to Rick Rinehart, who never lost his sense of humor.

Barbara Dittl
Joanne Mallmann

Interior, ca. 1900. Courtesy of the Haynes Foundation Collection, Montana State Historical Society

Foreword

It has been almost seventy years since my first visit to Yellowstone's Lake Hotel, and I remember it well. I can close my eyes and recall a warm, summer night with Lake Yellowstone shimmering against the backdrop of the distant Absarokas. The dining room windows are open to catch the breeze, and soft, indirect lights reflect on white linen, silver and crystal. Young college girls employed as waitresses hurry from kitchen to table with the fine food. In the distance, the music of a small instrumental group is heard in the lounge. Later on, when there is dancing, the ensemble will become a full fledged orchestra, some of the members having been bellhops or dishwashers earlier in the day. The young people do double duty at no extra pay. It is just fun!

One of the last times I spent a few days at Lake Hotel was in 1927 when President Calvin Coolidge and his family visited the Park. The President's wife and son John ate in the dining room and attended the entertainment and dancing later. Coolidge, a very private man, had me stay with him to discuss "important" presidential matters, and we sat in the corner of the lovely, newly furnished addition to the hotel. We settled ourselves in comfortable wicker chairs. His, a rocker, had beside it a convenient standing ashtray, as he was an inveterate cigar smoker (but mainly in private and never offering one to anyone else). After a lengthy silence, he said he had come to a decision. I hoped it was about my suggestion for adding the lovely Teton mountain area to Yellowstone or some such vital question. Not so. Coolidge stated that he wanted to change the itinerary to stay one more day at Lake Hotel so he could take in a new fishing area that sounded good.

I hope this book on a segment of Yellowstone Park's history will bring back memories to you as poignant as they are to me. If you have never been in the lounge (beautifully restored to its 1920s grandeur), reading this little history of the hotel, sipping a refreshing beverage, listening to the string quartet, and occasionally gazing at the snow-capped mountains across Lake Yellowstone, now is the time to go. Don't miss the experience.

Horace M. Albright
January 20, 1986

To maximize its Park profits, the Northern Pacific built hostelries at various points of interest along Yellowstone's Grand Loop Road. The Lake (shown above in 1891), Fountain, and original Canyon hotels were constructed simultaneously, each with on-site variations to the Railroad's generic floor plan. The photo at right shows the Lake Hotel during the final stages of construction in the Spring of 1891; the building's rubblestone walk is clearly visible, as is the widow's walk, removed during a later renovation. Courtesy of the Haynes Foundation Collection, Montana State Historical Society

From Plain to Fancy

EARLY in the 1880s the Northern Pacific Railroad realized Yellowstone's tourist potential. With its track extended westward into Montana, the Northern Pacific held a near monopoly on travel to and from the Park and had an interest in the stagecoach concessions within Yellowstone.

At various points around the Park, along the Grand Loop Road, the Railroad planned to erect hotels, a day's journey apart by horse-drawn vehicle, where travelers could spend the night. One of the stops was to be near the outlet of Yellowstone Lake, long known as a camping spot and meeting place for Indians, trappers, and mountain men.

In 1886 the Department of the Interior issued Charles Gibson a lease for a piece of land two miles west of the lower Yellowstone River. Gibson and his partners in the Yellowstone Park Association obtained financing from the Northern Pacific, but several years of stalling, squabbling, and excuses delayed the hotel's construction.

Work finally began in the spring of 1889. Wood was plentiful and a sawmill was erected at the hotel site. When lumbermen cutting timber for the structure were responsible for at least one large blaze ignited by sparks from their untended campfire, Superintendent Frazier Boutelle feared that "A single fire would entirely destroy the beauty of . . . one of the most delightful summer-hotel sites in the world."

Boutelle predicted in his 1889 annual report that the building would be ready for the 1890 season. To insure that outcome, Gibson ordered his YPA General Manager E. C. Waters to ". . . cover in the dining room floor and lathe it and the ell—and weather board them on the outside. . . . put that part of this hotel in a condition to be finished early in the Spring, so as to be ready for next season's business."

Native stone had been brought in by wagon from the surrounding area for the footings, but during a routine inspection in mid-November the YPA Controller made a disturbing discovery and wrote of it to Northern Pacific Railroad headquarters, saying, "I am told . . . that . . . there are many places in the foundation that [one] can today push over with his foot." In reply, Waters defended the Hotel as "well built & a splendid house for the money."

By the spring of 1890 the Yellowstone Park Association had modified its original plans by reducing the number of rooms and deleting require-

ments for mortised and tennoned joints, and re-mortared the worst sections of the rubblestone foundation.

Carpenters raised the frame by July 6 of that year, and manufactured materials were ordered through railroad headquarters in St. Paul, Minnesota. But deliveries were often incomplete, and there wasn't enough iron roofing to cover the completed section. The order for steam pipe arrived short by 200 feet. The shipment for electrical wire had not been received, and only part of the oak stairway had been sent from St. Paul. An October message to the Northern Pacific Purchasing Agent inquired, "Have not received door numbers for Lake order placed by you Sept 18th, when may I expect them?"

Despite mixups and mishaps, the Lake Hotel opened in 1891 and resembled other hotels built along the railroad rights of way with a flat-faced front, yellow clapboard exterior, and windows with black-painted trim. There was a veranda at the building's east end, with a porch on top of it, whose double doors opened onto a second floor parlor with a fireplace. There was a gable at each end of the roof. An observation deck, or widow's walk, sat atop the east gable.

> *". . . please send as soon as possible good plasterers wages $3.50 per day and board to take place of dissatisfied whiskey fiends."*
>
> NPRR telegram to W. G. Pearce 6/24/1890 from W. G. Johnson.

The Hotel's interior walls were finished with lead paint, and the flooring was mostly pine with a bit of oak in the stairway. The building used steam heat and electric lighting, and each bedroom door had a jet doorknob, rubber-tipped doorstop, and a glass transom.

Arriving from Minneapolis to work at the new Lake Hotel was Clara Green, 22, a Norwegian immigrant. Her 1891 diary has been lost, but an April 1892 entry tells of the "information about Yellowstone Park jobs, possibly in the restaurant of Lake Hotel. . . . "

Miss Green departed the Twin Cities on May 26. "At 11 o clock . . . I left home for the last time and went to the Mpls-St Paul depot. . . . A Minneapolis bunch left the depot at 4:15 PM. We friends all were together, so the first evening was enjoyable. Could sit and look out the window. Went over the endless Dakota prairie. . . . Got to Livingston 9 o clock Sat AM."

Photographer Elliott W. Hunter assembled this group of Lake and Canyon Hotel employees shortly after their arrival in the Park in June 1904. Haynes Collection, MHS

Miss Green and her companion travelers made a side trip to the Grand Canyon of the Yellowstone on June 2. On June 4 the entourage "Left at 9 o clock for the Lake. . . . had to jump out of the wagon every 10 steps. The snow was very deep some places[;] our feet . . . all wet. When we got here at 5 o clock, We were thankful we got here after all the trouble we had. Got my old room back. . . . "

In 1893 Superintendent George Anderson called the Lake "one of the pleasantest, best kept hotels in the Park," which he felt deserved more business than it was getting. To encourage additional customers, the YPA lowered its daily room rate from $4 to $3 after a stay of six days.

Said Anderson, "I see no reason why a 'stay in the Park,' rather than a 'tour of the Park,' should not be the rule."

The Superintendent did take issue with another Yellowstone stipulation, Rule Number 9, which stated, "No drinking saloon or bar room will be permitted within the limits of the Park." Anderson, while bound to uphold the law, was by no means a teetotaler and argued that spiritous liquors should be available, since "most of the waters of the Park affect the bowels of many tourists and the most temperate need brandy medicinally."

In 1895 Anderson ordered the YPA to convert two adjoining rooms on the Hotel's first floor into an area for mixing and serving drinks. He directed that a doorway be cut through the common wall so waiters would not be carrying alcoholic beverages in the main hallways.

Glass globes filled with carbon tetrachloride were the Hotel's earliest fire extinguishers. Some were suspended by fuseable wire, others were simply tossed into the blaze—thus the name "grenade extinguisher." Author photo

Only three years after its debut, the Hotel's roof began to leak. A letter written to Railroad headquarters described the problem. "The style of roofs used on all the principal buildings is the . . . V crimp roofing. As the vertical seams do not form a lock, the leaks occur principally at those seams during a driving rain, and when there is snow on the roofs which is liable to back up the water. I do not know of any cheaper way to repair the roofs . . . than to mop a strip of six or eight ounce duck over all the leaking spams [sic], coating it well with a paint made of coal tar and asphaltum."

In 1899 YPA Manager J. H. Dean complained that the Lake Hotel was losing business due to inadequate facilities. For years Charles Gibson had argued that the Northern Pacific kept room rates so low that profit, and expansion, were impossible. Weary of the hotel business and plagued with its own financial woes, the Railroad decided to sell the Yellowstone Park Association.

Several people tried to raise the money to buy the YPA, among them E. C. Waters. He failed, but Harry Child, a Montana banker, and two others succeeded in 1901 with a loan obtained from a Northern Pacific holding company. Four years later Child and the Railroad became co-owners of the Association. Waters, ever the spoiler, howled monopoly and lawsuit. The NP, wanting to avoid an inquiry, sold the rest of its stock to Child, who owned the Association outright but remained heavily in debt to the Railroad.

In the midst of these maneuverings, Child had begun an ambitious remodeling job on the Lake Hotel, with Robert Reamer as his architect. The two had met in California and traveled to the Park a few years earlier, although Reamer's daughter, Jane White, theorized, "It's possible that Dad visited Yellowstone as early as 1895."

In 1893 a team driver who had earned $35 a month hauling rock for the Hotel's foundation claimed that E. C. Waters had cheated him out of eighteen days' pay. The young man wrote the Acting Park Superintendent, "I thought waters was an honest man. His last letter was fraud. i will have it [my pay] or rise from my grave for revenge. . . . your friend, Jno [John] Spangler."

Ltr. John Spangler to Y.P. Superintendent, Nov. 10, 1893.

Robert Charles Reamer (at left and with daughter Jane, right), architect for several renovations to the Lake Hotel, was born September 12, 1873, in Oberlin, Ohio, and began his self-directed education at 13. Reamer worked in Chicago before moving to southern California, where he met Harry W. Child, President of the Yellowstone Park Association. Courtesy of Jane Reamer White

With his plan for the Lake Hotel Reamer created an oasis for guests who had traveled miles through thin air and thick dust. He used columns, gables, and decorative moldings to give an impression of neoclassical elegance. He extended the roofline at three places, adding fifty-foot ionic columns with fanlight windows in the roof projections. Reamer altered the window style and attached fifteen false balconies to those on the third floor. He designed a section which extended farther east than the original plan and added an ell to the rear of the building.

The new look contributed to a flurry of suggestions for renaming the structure, among them the Lake House and the Lake Colonial Hotel. But the Lake Hotel remained the Lake Hotel.

The Northern Pacific, though not directly involved with accommodations, was still interested in carrying passengers to Yellowstone. Railroad employees wrote promotional brochures for trips west, including descriptions of what their clients could expect.

In 1910 Passenger Agent A. M. Cleland wrote, "The reception-room [of the Lake Hotel] . . . is very large, finished in California redwood, electrically lighted at night. . . . It is a place where one feels wonderfully at home from the start. . . . "

On August 1, 1915, the first passenger cars legally drove into the Park. Visitors to Yellowstone were never again ferried automatically to a hotel for their night's lodging on their way around the Loop, but divided their time between inside accommodations and roughing it in the newly finished automobile camps.

By manipulating stagecoach traffic along the Grand Loop Road, E. C. Waters coerced Park tourists into buying his one-way steamboat tickets from West Thumb to Lake Hotel for $2.50 each. Waters also charged visitor Carl Schmidt $12 for a fishing trip starting at Lake Hotel, prompting Schmidt's comment, ". . . the only satisfaction I had was in telling him that I now knew why Christ walked on the water, that in the face of such charges anybody else would walk that was able to."

Carl E. Schmidt, *A Western Trip,* privately published, 1901.

When Reamer drew the elevations for his first remodeling of the Lake Hotel in 1904-05, neoclassicism was the prevailing architectural style. Roof dormers, Ionic columns, fanlight windows, and massive wrought iron coach lamps transformed the flat-faced railroad hostelry into a premier resort hotel. MHS

Bouquets of wildflowers graced dining room tables at the Lake Hotel in 1916. Stick reed ribband backed chairs, executed in birch, reflected the style of the day. An inventory of dining room furnishings also listed ivory painted serving stands and two bentwood high chairs. Haynes Collection, MHS

On August 25, 1916, President Woodrow Wilson signed the National Park Service into existence, and in April 1917 the United States entered World War I. With all available labor and monies diverted to the war effort, Superintendent Horace M. Albright estimated that attendance "dropped . . . to somewhere around 18,000 people, and that included all the local people that came in from around there to fish and so forth."

The Lake Hotel was closed during 1918 and 1919, but in September of that year repairs were begun to ready the building for the following summer. Superintendent Albright reported, "At the Lake Hotel the improvements that will be the most noteworthy will include a porte-cochere in front of the central entrance . . . built with faithful adherence to the colonial architecture. . . . The old porch floors will be replaced by concrete walks." These improvements enabled touring cars and buses to drop off passengers and baggage lakeside without regard for the weather.

In 1922 the Yellowstone Park Association concession agreement was up for renewal. Interior Secretary Albert B. Fall bluntly told Harry Child, "I think you will be entitled to new contracts . . . if you build the new Lake Hotel this year. . . . "

Fortunately for Child, National Park Service Director Stephen Mather had coincidentally approved plans for an annex to the Hotel, which, again, Robert Reamer had designed. Reamer's elevations called for a 122-bedroom, four-story extension attached to the existing structure by an atrium-like glass enclosure. Between blueprints and building, he reduced the number of rooms and changed the wing connection to wooden frame construction, with a battery-powered elevator installed in the area.

Workmen encountered a geological obstruction while digging the footings, and compensated by building the annex at a slight angle from the original structure. They also replaced the first floor's easternmost section with a half-height storage area, maintaining the wing's appearance of four full floors.

In 1910 Harry Child had enlarged the Hotel's dining room, but by 1920 diners were complaining of "head waiters who sold preference . . . when crowds were so great as to require two or three sittings." In 1924 Child replaced the old dining area with one that would seat 400.

The project also included utilizing the space over the dining hall. These rooms came to be known as the Presidential Suite, possibly as much for Harry Child's staying in them as their availability to later U.S. Presidents. It was a good place to escape the "touri," as Mrs. Harry Child referred to the automobile travelers.

Marion Sanger, Child's granddaughter, remembered, "He [Child] would put us . . . children and our three Nichols cousins, along with a suitable chaperone, into an open 11 passenger White touring bus and he would lead the way in his Lincoln Phaeton to 'make the loop.' We always spent the second night at Lake Hotel where he had us put in several rooms at the very end of the long wing to the right of the lakeside entrance, and he went up to the 'presidential suite' at the far left."

During 1923 and 1924 Robert Reamer extensively remodeled the Hotel's lobby, directing that the redwood paneling and posts be painted white, and ordering new furniture from H. von Briesen of San Francisco. With his concern for any project's total effect, it is probable that Reamer chose the pieces himself.

The focal point of this renovation was the fireplace and mantel facing installed on the lobby's rear wall. The style has been identified as Rookwood, and Herbert Peck, an authority on this art form, has said, "The mantel facing . . . was unquestionably designed as a special job for Yellowstone. . . . "

Robert Reamer designed the Hotel's fireplace, installed in 1923 and reset in 1984. Its dimensions were substantial: 17 feet 10 inches wide by 7 feet 10 inches high. Diamond-shaped tiles (*above, center*) showed a pine cone spray motif; at each side of the firebox a large panel depicted a forest scene (*left*). To the right of the hearth Reamer added a wall-hung drinking fountain that restated the design of the fireplace panels with an elk standing majestically before a pine forest.

The sand jar (*left*), whose replacement value in 1929 was listed as all of $3, was executed in the same matte glazes used in the fireplace installation. The jar was rediscovered in the early 1980s and returned to the hearthside assemblage. Author photos

Executed by unknown craftsmen, the fireplace design was created by Park architect Reamer, who had a habit of sketching details on anything handy—a roof shingle, piece of paper, or scrap of wood—choosing the design he liked best, and expecting the workmen to effect the end result.

At the east end of the lobby Reamer removed fifteen sleeping rooms, installed a newsstand next to the stairs, and established an area nearby for the sale of photographic supplies and Haynes's Yellowstone post cards. Next to this was the telegraph desk, and beyond that the porter's room.

A bit farther down the hall was the dispensary, staffed by on-duty nurses and doctors who checked in periodically. The room contained several tables, bath stools, side chairs, a mohair couch, and an electric grill. Many of the injuries treated were ankle sprains, and two pairs of

In 1926 when this picture was taken, one ring meant bell boy, two meant ice water, and three rings meant baggage out. Haynes Collection, MHS

crutches, valued at seven dollars, were kept at the ready in the checkroom.

Reamer relocated the registration desk in a remodeled guest room on the lake side of the building, placed an office next to that, and added a grillroom farther along that could be entered from the porch.

Although much attention had been given to the remodeling of the Hotel's facade and first floor, the upper sleeping rooms retained their utilitarian character. The spartan decor was enhanced only by glass pitchers, tumblers, and trays, and according to Marion Child Sanger, "Each room had bedspreads of beige cotton, sheer curtains at the windows, and wool blankets in russet, green, or Yellowstone yellow."

In 1926 the Crown Prince and Princess of Sweden visited the Park, and because the Prince was an inveterate fisherman, the royal couple sojourned at Lake Hotel. Superintendent and Mrs. Albright hosted the couple personally, and Mrs. Albright planned a special dinner in their honor, decorating the hotel dining room with a wilderness theme, enhanced by small trees and shrubs from the Lake area, animals borrowed from various Park museum exhibits, and bouquets of Yellowstone wildflowers.

The royal entourage entered the dining room according to protocol, Albright remembered, with Mrs. Albright "going in on the arm of the

Crown Prince, the Crown Princess on the arm of the Secretary of the Interior, the lady-in-waiting [with] the head of the Park Service, the chief of the Swedish army, the Swedish ambassador, the Governor of Montana, and here was [Albright] the Superintendent of Yellowstone, back with the waiters."

In 1927 President and Mrs. Calvin Coolidge stayed at the Lake Hotel, and in 1928 Robert Reamer drafted plans for the Lake's last major addition. He enlarged the lobby area by removing the remaining guest rooms between the dining hall and registration desk, and eliminating the bar and wine rooms. He relocated the photo shop and newsstand and enclosed part of the original porte cochere. Reamer built a new covered porch just east of that section and integrated this addition with the existing lobby. He designed more than seventy art glass light fixtures for the area and replaced the stairway's Victorian balusters and newel post with those in the Colonial style.

The Yellowstone Park Company hired students from Montana State University in Bozeman to chauffeur tourists through the Park. This fleet, collecting passengers at the Lake Hotel, drove sightseers to various points of interest along the Park's Grand Loop Road. To the right is a horse-drawn vehicle from Yellowstone's stagecoach days. Haynes Collection, MHS

In 1890 the Bohn Manufacturing Company of St. Paul supplied oak balusters for the Lake Hotel. In 1928 Robert Reamer replaced those on the first floor with a newel post and complementary woodwork in the colonial style. Author photo

To the south of the lobby, Reamer added a lounge that extended toward Yellowstone Lake. Large areas of glass offered visitors tranquil yet dynamic views toward Sylvan Pass, the Teton Range, and the Heart Lake–Mt. Sheridan area. With its mahogany grand piano and conversational furniture groupings, the room had a solarium atmosphere enhanced by a set of draperies designed by Margaret Goodwin, an artist whose husband was the head of Yellowstone Park Lodge and Camps Company.

Isabel M. Haynes remembered that the draperies, originally designed by Mrs. Goodwin for Mammoth Lodge, had patterns silk screened onto a cream mohair background and represented ". . . the YNP wildflowers. Arnica Daisy . . . Lupine . . . Paint Brush . . . some stems with seeds . . . showy flowers that she enlarged and elongated."

With this new look, Reamer finished the Lake Hotel's transformation from a nineteenth century railroad hostelry to a twentieth century resort hotel. But four years later in 1932 people were out of work and had little money for travel to the wilderness. For the second time in its history, the Lake Hotel closed.

In 1936 the lodging concessionaires merged to form the Yellowstone Park Company, which assumed sole responsibility for overnight accommodations, cafeterias, transportation, and the woodselling operation.

In their free time, YP Company employees celebrated a full calendar year of holidays during the three-month Yellowstone season. This 1938 affair, complete with Betty Boop dolls, was photographed in the lounge of the Lake Hotel. Haynes Collection, MHS

BOOZE CLEANED UP

Bootlegging Cut Short Lake Hotel Scene of Attempted Operations—Rangers and Hotel Authorities Cooperate

Six days after bootlegging operations were begun at the Lake hotel, the five men chiefly involved were arrested by ranger sleuths on the trail and 16 days after that they were brought to trial and fined a total of $600 and costs by the United States department of justice.

Hotel authorities co-operated with the administration in clearing up the law violations, which were attempted by outsiders and employes on their own hook.

Brought before Judge John W. Meldrum, representing the United States department of justice at Mammoth, those involved pleaded guilty of violation of the Volstead act (nineteenth constitutional amendment), and were fined as follows:

Frank J. White, assistant manager of the Lake hotel—$150.
Thomas D. Dwyer, head porter—$150.
R. J. Wells, front clerk—$100.
W. H. Gruenhagen, bellboy—$100.
Otto J. Breil, porter—$100.

Tourist Tattler, vol. I, No. IX, last number of the Year, 1921.

Travel to the Park increased that year as the economy improved, and Yellowstone officials hoped to greet half a million visitors. Vacationers arrived by train, trailer houses, and private automobiles, and for the second year in a row National Park Airways flew tourists into West Yellowstone.

Then as now the Yellowstone season comprised mainly June, July, and August, and a good portion of any year's revenue was reinvested in building maintenance. After deciding to reopen the Lake Hotel in 1937, the YP Company ordered the roof reshingled and the building repainted in its familiar yellow. The power plant's boilers, which had originally driven the tourist boat "E. C. Waters" and used as many as 535 cords of wood to provide steam for the Hotel, were converted to the use of oil.

Interior upkeep was also expensive. The Company contained costs wherever possible, purchasing only necessary items such as ranges,

ovens, coffee urns for the kitchen, and ten chenille bedspreads for the linen supply.

During 1940 workmen ripped up carpeting at Lake, tacked it down in the east wing of the Old Faithful Inn, and resettled over one hundred twin beds at the same location. These furnishings were taken from the Lake Hotel's rear wing, added by Reamer in 1903-04 and razed in 1940.

As Huntley Child, Jr. recounted, "Before the War, we persuaded ourselves that what we wanted . . . was a comparatively modest hotel and cottages, . . . and in a spirit of joie de vivre, we gaily tore down the wing we built in 1903, thereby destroying some fifty or sixty perfectly good rooms. . . . The cottages back of the hotel were started in 1941, then the War came. . . ."

Lake Hotel closed for the third time from 1942 through 1946. Early figures for May 1945 had indicated an increase in summer travelers to Yellowstone, and over that winter the YP Company decided to reopen some of the hotels and lodges for the first post-war season. However, Superintendent Edmund Rogers lamented that ". . . it was not possible to have all operations opened on schedule because of the scarcity of materials and the general attitude of labor expecting to receive high wages with little work. Positions were difficult to fill and food supplies were hard to obtain." The Lake Hotel provided sleeping accommodations only during July and August 1947.

As statistics had begun to show before World War II, more visitors were arriving by family auto or house trailer than by common carrier. These travelers wanted different levels of accommodation, from tent camping to cabins to hotel rooms. But meager wartime revenues, coupled with continuing financial obligations, made it difficult for the YP Company to build additional facilities while upgrading their existing structures.

In partial compliance with its 1955 contract renewal, the Yellowstone Park Company rehabilitated fifty-three private rooms and eight public lavatories and hallways in the Lake Hotel's east wing, and updated the kitchen and dining room. Huntley Child, Jr. also recalled that during the early 1950s ". . . serious thought was given to cutting through the hotel east of the center porte cochere . . ." for an automobile drive-through.

The company even considered razing Lake Hotel and combining its facilities with those at Lake Lodge, but decided against this. Instead they remodeled an additional eighty rooms in the east wing, and changed the first floor decor to birch veneer moderne, replacing the solarium ambience of the 1920s with a starkness pervasive in the 1950s. The Company

Until the early 1980s, the Lake Hotel provided the entire Park with its ice supply. The flat-roofed structure (*top photo*) partially hidden by pine trees held the ammonia coils and ice-making bins, removed in 1985. At the picture's extreme left is the original rear wing of the Hotel, razed in 1940. *Bottom* In 1950 the Lake Hotel curio shop and photo stand were located on the lobby's north wall, opposite the Reamer lounge. Later the shop was moved to make room for the Drydock Lounge, but the Park Service gutted the bar area in 1984 and returned the gift shop to its former site. Haynes Collection, MHS

In preparation for a tourist season in the late 1950s, the Yellowstone Park Company engaged a firm to give the Lake Hotel a fresh coat of paint. Just as the crew finished spraying the building, a strong southeast wind plastered a newly hatched crop of snowflies to the wet clapboards. Thomas J. Hallin, former Y.P. Company Vice President, recalled, "They literally covered the hotel. It was just black. We had to . . . scrape and sand all that off and redo it." Courtesy of Jerry Bateson, Sr.

tried to attract visitors to these accommodations at the Lake, but profits declined, ending with a poor year in 1958.

The 1959 season promised to reverse that trend, when on August 17 at 11:37 p.m. a strong earthquake shook the Park. Some plaster dropped in the Hotel's hallways, and it was later learned that the fireplace's mantel had become dislodged from the wall by several inches.

Although visible damage to the Hotel was minimal, the tremor terrified guests. Jerry Bateson, a former Hotel winterkeeper, remembered that "things really started shakin'. . . . the people were scared. . . . a lot of 'em wanted to leave. . . . And the rest . . . just stretched out on the floor in the lobby and stayed down there. They were afraid to go to their rooms."

Mark Hargis, previously head of maintenance at the Hotel, recalled that people checked out still wearing their nightclothes, drove as far as they could, found that the Park Service had closed the roads, and had to check in again on the morning of the 18th. What had begun as a promising summer for the Yellowstone Park Company coffers ended with visitors departing prematurely, and others, who had planned to stay in the

Park, avoiding the Yellowstone area, which reduced house counts and revenues substantially.

In addition to the natural and financial setbacks, Harry Child's descendants, as stockholders and officers of the YP Company, were plagued by falling receipts and rising maintenance costs, and the probability of having to commit scarce dollars to the Park's development at Grant Village. In 1965 the family sold its possessory interests in the Yellowstone Park Company to Goldfield Enterprises, soon bought out by General Host Corporation.

In 1972 the nation's first national park celebrated its 100th birthday. Preparations for the centennial had included rerouting the Grand Loop road between Fishing Bridge and Bridge Bay, bypassing the traditional Lake Hotel approach. Instead tour buses deposited visitors at the building's back door, where a makeshift canopy gave way to a dingy interior with faded hall runners and lackluster guest rooms. Framed maps and posters disappeared from lounge walls, and the furniture was mismatched and threadbare. The hotel's kitchen and dining room slipped well below code requirements, and employee morale plummeted.

Seasonal workers resented their low wages, long hours, unsatisfactory working conditions, and crowded employee accommodations. Many made their dissatisfaction apparent to Hotel guests, who in turn protested to the Park Superintendent about surly employees, unappetizing food, and lumpy beds.

In a dramatic and decisive confrontation, the National Park Service cancelled General Host's contract on October 31, 1979, and purchased all assets belonging to the former YP Company. The NPS then agreed upon a two-year interim arrangement with TW Services, which embarked on an ambitious program to stem tourist complaints and restore quality guest facilities and services to Yellowstone. TW imported a staff trained in concessions management with an emphasis in the food and beverage areas.

TW's next commitment during the winter of 1980-81 was to update old-fashioned fire and security systems, necessary changes that few guests would notice. The corporation installed fire-rated chip board, replaced the original jet hardware with brass doorknobs, nailed up the transoms, and hung new exit doors.

During the following winter, Richard Engle, an engineer with the National Park Service, oversaw additional renovation in the east wing where "the top floors were still in a straight line, but that first floor [was] an inch and a half out of plumb." Thirty years earlier Huntley Child, Jr. had said of this phenomenon, "Going down the halls of these floors was like riding a rollacoaster."

Engle theorized that this waviness had occurred soon after the wing's construction in 1923. Reamer's plans had called for all the floors to have the same configuration, with doors and windows stacked above one another, creating a structural weakness so that "all the movement took place in the [doorways]. . . . the new [doors] were cut to fit the out-of-plumb frames."

Workmen hired for various construction projects often found messages long concealed by layers of plaster and paint. During the 1980-81 remodeling of the building's east wing, Park Service Engineer Dick Engle saw a caricature penned in a style almost certainly that of architect Robert Reamer. Author photo

Despite this assessment, Engle was impressed with the quality of Reamer's addition. "The surprising thing we found about the east wing was the differences in construction. If you looked at the very oldest part of the hotel, . . . the trim around the windows and doors [was] minimal, just planks, just plaster walls and so-so construction. . . .

"[In the east wing] in between each room [was] a double studded 2 × 6 wall . . . [with] studs that [were] staggered . . . so that you [didn't] have sound going directly through. It was a fairly expensive way to go. . . . And the wood [was] quite hard. The trim and all the rest of it was pretty fancy. . . . [Where possible] all the old trim was put back on. . . ."

Outdoor readings for the winter of 1981-82 skidded to minus forty-five degrees, and by mid-January the unheated parts of the hotel registered 0 degrees to minus ten. When it came time for the crew to repaint the interior walls, the workmen used portable electric heaters to warm nineteen rooms at a time. Although the inside temperature reached seventy degrees Fahrenheit, strong lake winds blowing through the cracks in the siding froze the paint to the walls as soon as the workers applied it.

TW completed its first full year under long-term contract in 1981, reinvesting twenty-two percent of gross revenues and all pretax profits in excess of five percent in repair, maintenance, and capital improvements. By June of 1983 the Lake Hotel kitchen had been transformed from a dour, inefficient facility to a gleaming network of food preparation stations fashioned of stainless steel and ceramic tile. TW also gutted and rebuilt the first floor washrooms, made long overdue foundation repairs, and remodeled the employees' dining room.

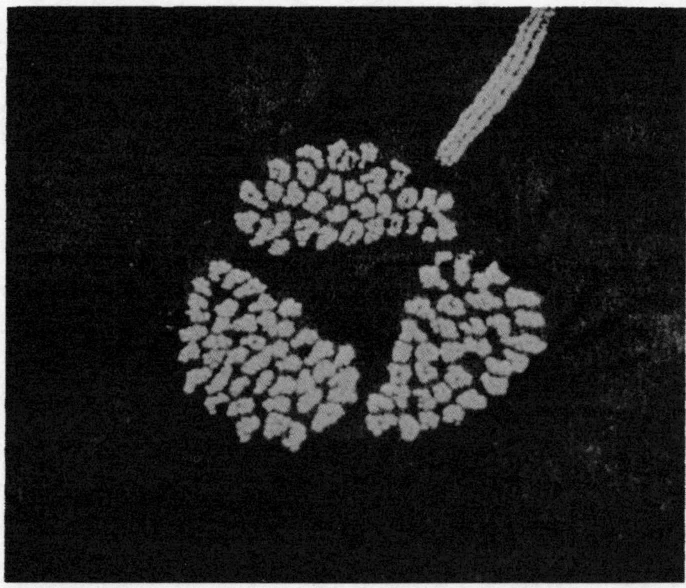

New area rugs in Contemporary Mauve or Inspiration Green were installed throughout the lobby and lounge during the 1984-85 redecoration. The design recalled Reamer's diamond-shaped fireplace tiles, and were loomed to match pine boughs sent from the Park. Author photo

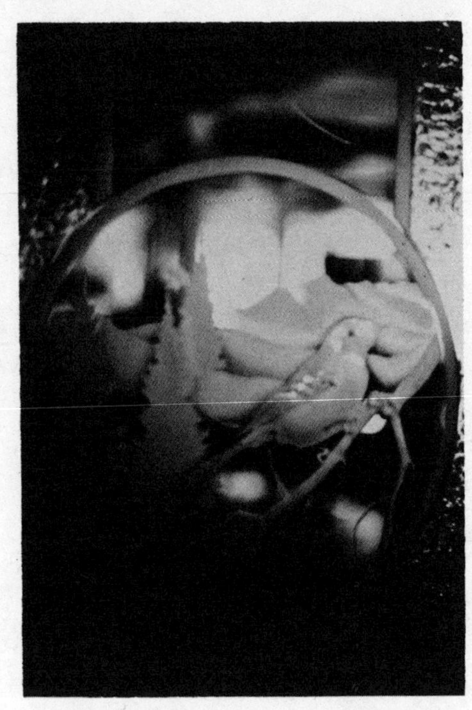

Kersey's carved glass of Hayward, California effected the delicacy of quaking aspen, wildflower likenesses, and the textures of fur and feather in glass by employing a sequential process of line drawing, sand blasting, carving, and polishing. By a process known as glue chipping Kersey's framed these scenes with edgings suggestive of shaved ice. Author photo

Coincident with these projects, TW worked with the National Park Service and Spencer Associates to refurbish the Hotel's lobby, lounge, and dining room. The principals agreed that contemporary standards of good taste had to be considered, and, with a relative abundance of furniture and appointments from the 1920s, settled on that period—or, as Park historian Timothy Manns put it, ". . . what we'd like to think of as the 1920s."

Working in conjunction with the TW/Spencer overall plan, the National Park Service located the new gift shop to the left of the fireplace, in the site of the former Drydock Lounge. Dating from the early 1950s, the Lounge had been a secluded alcove with cocktail tables, minimal lighting, and blackened windows. The Park Service changed this to a sales area of clear display cases and windows, pale carpeting, and walls repainted in Whisper White gloss. It replaced the Lounge's dropped shadow box ceiling and saloon-type entrance with track-based spotlights and double doors with etched glass panels.

Executed by Kersey's Carved Glass of Hayward, California, the door inserts were two of thirty-three partitions designed for the Lake Hotel. Kersey's worked from personal memories and Park photographs to recreate Yellowstone scenes, such as a trout leaping to capture a dragonfly, a frieze of running bison, a chickadee resting on a branch. Kersey's installed the largest glass panel to the right of the new bar at the dining room entrance. The scene showed a bull elk, its antlers polished and neck thickened, listening for a challenger's bugling reply.

The 1929 American Appraisal inventory of the Lake Hotel documented the furniture shown in the Haynes photograph above, including writing tables and plant stands. The frugality of the Yellowstone Park Company in storing these and other pieces insured the authenticity of the 1985 lobby and lounge renovation (*below*).

During this project TW established a furniture refinishing shop, and one employee remarked that the old wing chairs, arm chairs, and settees had been recovered so many times that it was difficult to find a new place on which to secure a tack. The color scheme chosen for the redecoration combined deep rose with forest greens and palest mauves, and complementary shades were also used in the dining room. There chairs were finished in Honeytone Teak and Raspberry, and deeply glossed mauve tables reflected the area's subdued lighting. Author photo

Spencer's Harry Rhodda, AIA, saw these installations as one of the unifying themes in the refurbishing of the first floor, leading visitors from the registration desk to the gift shop and on to the dining room, where white Shenango china, Embassy glassware, and stainless flatware provided a neutral background for appetizing, attractively served meals.

In the remodeling of the dining, lobby, and lounge areas, Rhodda decided to work "primarily with paint to enliven the walls and ceilings, with magnificent rugs and carpets, and to change the light fixtures to provide a more emphatic lighting statement." Spencer replaced the Reamer-designed art glass lighting with gooseneck wall lamps, the style of which hinted at the Hotel's very earliest designs.

The decorators opted for an ambience of sophisticated relaxation, choosing chandeliers in a style complementary to that of the rooms' bracket lights. TW tinted the ceilings Orange Shake and the beams Whisper White and Sweet Apricot, and painted the support columns Granada Rose and touched the decorative moldings with, again, Whisper White. The window treatments repeated this theme, and the area's baseboard and column moldings concluded the effect in a color known simply as Ink.

TW integrated the refurbished chairs and sofas with modern cubi and parsons tables, combining pale wicker with plastic laminate in Surf and Rosedust, completing the old-new effect with lush Boston ferns, wicker plant stands, and polished hardwood floors.

In June 1984 TW hosted a reception at the Lake Hotel to celebrate the completion of this first phase of the building's adaptive restoration. Invited to the event were many of the people who had contributed to the project.

With plans to complete the building's rejuvenation by its 1991 centennial, the hotel is regaining the reputation it enjoyed in the early 1900s. The Lake Hotel is the oldest hostelry in Yellowstone today, a dowager survivor in America's premier park.

Haynes Collection, MHS

References

Oral History Interviews

Horace M. Albright
Jerry Bateson, Sr.
John Burchill
Huntley Child, Jr.
John Delmar
Dick and Rosemary Engle
Aubrey L. Haines
Thomas J. Hallin
Mark Hargis
Charles Hudson
Isabel M. Haynes
Steve Kersey
John King
Timothy Manns
Verne Moss
Tom Nelson
Ellie and Trevor Povah
Harry Rhodda
Marian Albright Schenck
Marion Child Sanger
Dave Smith
George Swim
Steve Tedder
Jean Ward
Mark Watson
Rodd Wheaton
Jane Reamer White

Libraries and Historical Societies

Colorado State Historical Society, Denver, Colorado
Custer State Park, Badger Clark Hole Library, South Dakota
Denver Public Library, Western History Room, Denver, Colorado
Huntington Library, San Marino, California
Idaho State Historical Society, Boise, Idaho
Library of Congress, Washington, D.C.
Los Angeles Public Library, Los Angeles, California
Milwaukee Public Library, Milwaukee, Wisconsin
Minnesota Historical Society, St. Paul, Minnesota
Montana Historical Society, Helena, Montana
Montana State University Library, Bozeman, Montana
University of Wisconsin—Milwaukee Golda Meir Library, Milwaukee, Wisconsin
West Yellowstone Historical Society, West Yellowstone, Montana
Wyoming State Archives and History Department, Cheyenne, Wyoming
Yellowstone Association (Formerly the Yellowstone Library and Museum Association), Mammoth Hot Springs, Wyoming

Books

Albright, Horace Marden, and Taylor, Frank J. *"Oh Ranger!" A Book About the National Parks.* Revised edition, New York: Dodd, Mead & Co., 1934.

Albright, Horace Marden. *The Birth of the National Park Service: The Founding Years 1913-1933.* Salt Lake City: Howe Brothers, 1985.

Bartlett, Richard A. *Yellowstone: A Wilderness Besieged.* Tucson: University of Arizona Press, 1985.

Beal, Merril D. *The Story of Man in Yellowstone.* Caldwell, Idaho: Caxton Printers, 1949.

Chittenden, Hiram Martin. *The Yellowstone National Park.* Cincinnati: Steward & Kidd, 1915.

Haines, Aubrey L. *The Yellowstone Story.* Two vols. Boulder: Yellowstone Library and Museum Association with

Colorado Associated University Press, 1977.

Hampton, H. Duane. *How the U.S. Cavalry Saved Our National Parks.* Bloomington: Indiana University Press, 1971.

Kirk, Ruth. *Exploring Yellowstone.* Seattle: Yellowstone Library and Museum Association in cooperation with University of Washington Press, 1972.

Quick, Herbert. *Yellowstone Nights.* New York: Grosset and Dunlap, 1911.

Schmidt, Carl E. *A Western Trip.* Privately published, 1901.

Schullery, Paul, Editor. *Old Yellowstone Days.* Boulder: Colorado Associated University Press, 1979.

Wilson, Richard Guy, Editor. *Victorian Resorts and Hotels,* Vol. 8, Nos. 1-2, The Victorian Society in America, 1982.

Wirth, Conrad. *Parks, Politics, and the People.* Norman: University of Oklahoma Press, 1980.

Public Documents

Annual Reports of the Superintendents of Yellowstone National Park to the Secretary of the Interior, in *Reports of the Department of the Interior.* Washington, D.C.: Government Printing Office, for the years 1886 to 1982.

Battle, David G., and Thompson, Edwin N. Fort Yellowstone: Historical Structure Report. Denver Service Center: National Park Service, 1972.

Unpublished Materials

American Appraisal Company Inventory, 30 September 1929, vol. 4. Yellowstone National Park.

Clemensen, Berle, "Structural Study," National Park Service, Washington, D.C., n.d.

Green, Clara, "Comments on Working in Yellowstone National Park 1891-1892," diary. Yellowstone National Park.

Haynes Foundation Collection photographs and architectural drawing materials at Montana Historical Society. Helena, Montana.

Johnson, Mrs. Edward H., "Diary of a Trip Thru Yellowstone Park," Fort Dodge, Iowa, 1905. Yellowstone National Park.

Joyner, Newell F., "History of Improvements in Yellowstone National Park," 1929. Yellowstone National Park.

Kreisman, Larry, Biographical Sketch/ Architectural Survey of Robert Reamer for use in connection with a study of civic design and planning history in Seattle, Washington. n.d.

"Mission 66 for Yellowstone National Park," mimeographed prospectus of the National Park Service (circa 1956).

"Project Roche Jaune," compiled by Thomas J. Hallin, January 1, 1960. Yellowstone National Park.

United States Department of the Interior. "Yellowstone National Park Concessions Management Review of the Yellowstone Park Company." Washington: National Park Service 1977.

Newspapers and Periodicals

Atlantic Monthly
Billings Gazette
Business Week
Cody Enterprise
Dude Rancher
Gardiner Wonderland
Great Falls Tribune
Harper's Weekly
House and Garden
Ladies Home Journal
Literary Digest
Livingston Enterprise
Milwaukee Journal
Montana: The Magazine of Western History
Mountain Gazette
Nation
National Geographic
National Parks and Conservation Magazine
New York Times

Overland
Pacific Northwest Quarterly
Park County News
Reader's Digest
Scribner's
Tourist Tattler
Wonderland
Yellowstone Cub

Pamphlets

"A Gathering of Nations; A Time of Purpose." Centennial Celebration of Yellowstone and the Second World Conference on National Parks. 1972.

"Astonishing Yellowstone." 1937.

"Campbell's New Revised Complete Guide and Descriptive Book of the Yellowstone Park," Reau Campbell, Chicago, Illinois, 1909.

"Hamilton's Guides"

"Haynes' Guides"

"Motorist's Guide," Yellowstone National Park, USGS, 1927.

"Savage Special," Northern Pacific Railroad brochure, 1952.

"Shaw and Powell Camping Company," circa 1914.

"The Yellowstone Park," travel brochure, Burlington Route, 1910.

"Through Wonderland," A. M. Cleland, 1910.

"Yellowstone National Park," Northern Pacific Railroad brochure, 1907.

"Yellowstone Park," Yellowstone Park Company brochure, circa 1891.

Yellowstone Park Transportation Company brochure, 1905.

About The Authors

Barbara Dittl and Joanne Mallmann began collaborating ten years ago and published their initial work on Yellowstone's Lake Hotel in *Montana: The Magazine of Western History.* With backgrounds in English and Journalism, respectively, they have written and illustrated humorous articles for the Milwaukee *Sentinel.* In addition, their advice and etiquette column for cat lovers entitled *Ms. Meowser* appeared for three years in an east coast publication. They live with their families in Milwaukee, Wisconsin.